Woolgathering: Awareness of the Foreign in Published Works About Cowichan Woolworking

Paula Johanson

Published by Doublejoy Books, 2021.

WOOLGATHERING: AWARENESS OF THE FOREIGN IN PUBLISHED WORKS ABOUT COWICHAN WOOLWORKING

First edition. October 18, 2021.

ISBN: 978-1989966310

Written by Paula Johanson.

Table of Contents

Dedicated to May Sam, Elder for the First Peoples House at University of Victoria, with thanks for her kind support at my master's defense.

Acknowledgement

I acknowledge, as history scholar Sylvia Olsen does, the importance and difficulty of using appropriate names for people of Colonial and First Nations descent. The colonists cannot be called "Englishmen" because many were Scots and some were women; they weren't all European because many were Canadian or American-born or even of African descent. And that issue is the easiest dilemma of naming people in the subject of this paper, *Woolgathering*.

Like Olsen, literary scholar Alan Twigg uses the terms "First Nation" "Indian" "native" "indigenous" "aboriginal" "Coast Salish" "Salish" and "Siwash" in his book *Aboriginality* when each of these words is appropriate for the times and events being discussed. Words can change quickly or slowly, but courtesy is always appropriate. In this text, I hope to follow the examples set by Olsen, Twigg, and film-maker

Christine Welsh in using a variety of names – always with courteous intent and consideration for other people's perspectives.

Introduction

In the logbook from the Nootka portion of his 1778 voyage around the world, Captain James Cook recorded trading for "a sort of woollen stuff, or blanketing"[1]; Cook collected several woollen blankets woven by First Nations people of the Pacific Northwest coast in their traditional manner. The distinctive qualities of Cowichan woolworking have been remarked upon many times since, and understanding this history of commentary is a crucial step toward understanding the Cowichan sweater's place within non-Cowichan culture. On a January 2013 episode of CBC television's show *Dragon's Den*, for example, when Salish Fusion Knitworks pitched a business expansion plan, the "dragon" investors dismissed it as too small with the rude statement "How many grandmothers can you enslave?"; this reply carries with it a complex array of cultural assumptions about the Cowichan people, about First Nations peoples, and about woolworking. Woolworking has long been a primary cultural communication method of the Cowichan people, but as these comments suggest, non-Cowichan people have consistently failed to understand what was being communicated. When we examine the last 240 years of comments on Cowichan woolworking, whether published works by non-Cowichan authors primarily intended for non-Cowichan readers, or published works involving Cowichan participation, we see emphasized throughout the question of foreignness.

During this inquiry, I will compare and contrast the approaches of such works as official 19th-century colonial reports, 20th-century newspaper articles, 21st-century films and television, books by fibre arts professionals, and juried art shows accompanied by books based on artists' statements. These published works can be considered together as examples of an ongoing commentary, not only on the fabric-making of the Cowichan people but on the idea of foreignness, in a particularly West Coast manifestation. For each of these writers, their statements about Cowichan woolworking have been accompanied by their awareness of something foreign, by any of several definitions of the word "foreign." The speaker is aware of a different culture or country, subject to a different jurisdiction of law, and with different customs, where the people are different in appearance because of race and clothing as well as different in behaviours such as work, food preparation and home life – different, that is, from the speaker's own norms, or those of the intended reader. In the case of the Cowichan people, I am discussing here the gathering and processing of wool – first the wool of mountain goats and wool dogs and later the wool of sheep – by Cowichan woolworkers, in culturally specific ways anchored in the experience of a particular place.

Cowichan is the name of a bay and a fertile agricultural valley on the east shore of Vancouver Island, north of the city of Victoria and south of the city of Nanaimo, on the Pacific coast of Canada in the province of British Columbia. "The Northwest

Coast of North America was, for the English, the ocean's farthest shore," wrote historian Barry Gough.[2] Before the area was settled in 1862 by colonists backed up by Crown Colony gunboats, this bay and valley were already the home of several thousand First Nations people (Dorricott and Cullon 206-7). The Cowichan people are part of the Hul'qumi'num-speaking First Nations; Coast Salish is a term invented by anthropologists and linguists to describe one of several language groups on the Pacific northwest coast of North America, as fibre arts writer Paula Gustafson observed in her book *Salish Weaving* (Gustafson 17). On Vancouver Island, the Cowichan people are one of several groups who speak related dialects or languages in the Coast Salish language family, and there are other groups on the mainland in British Columbia and Washington state. While it is hard to determine how long Coast Salish people have lived in this part of the world[3], the middens under some of their village sites have accumulated gradually for several thousand years (Mackie n.p.). "The Cowichan believe that wool working goes as far back as the ice age," stated Sylvia Olsen in her landmark book *Working With Wool* (Olsen 35). The time of transition from traditional Coast Salish weaving to knitting among the Cowichan people was approximately 1855 to 1864; by the time of the 1858 Gold Rush, there was already little or no traditional weaving being done as settlers began moving into the Cowichan area. The production by Cowichan people of knitted goods for sale and for family use was underway by 1864 when the Sisters of Saint Anne founded a school in Cowichan, teaching girls and some of their parents how to knit and use spinning wheels instead of hand spindles, and that production continues to this day. Traditional weaving, in the latter part of the 20th century, saw a renewal through cultural exchanges with other Coast Salish groups and with other Indigenous weavers along the Pacific coast.

In this paper, I will show that during the last 240 years, the published works about Cowichan woolworking fall into three separate discourses in their ongoing commentary on foreignness: 1) the colonial discourse, from brief anthropological notes and comments, both by explorers and by Colonial authorities, to later commentary for general readers on traditional Coast Salish weaving and the development of the trade in knitted goods by Cowichan people in what was seen as a partially successful and ongoing assimilation to modern ways; 2) the fibre arts discourse, marked by a paradigm shift as fibre arts professionals and scholars published patterns and commentary on Cowichan woolworking and took pleasure in foreign qualities of this work; and 3) the indigenous discourse, visible in published works made by First Nations people or in very close consultation with them in the early years of the 21st century. There was some progression from one discourse to another, but for only a very few commentators, and in consequence these discourses remain distinct.

The rest of this paper will be written in three sections, about these three discourses. In the first section, I'll quote from commentary on Colonial records, academic works by Barbara Lane, Wilson Duff, and Margaret Meikle, and Northwest Pacific regional newspapers. In the second section, I will use as my references the books of Priscilla Gibson-Roberts, Lela Nargi and other fibre art professionals while discussing the origins of the iconic Cowichan Indian sweater, as well as the influence of Cowichan knitting on other knitters' work. In the third section, my sources will be Coast Salish artists, as quoted in the National Film Board documentary *The Story of the Coast Salish Knitters* (2008) and the books *Working With Wool*, *S'abadeb – The Gifts*, *Transporters I LECILEN*, *Time Warp*, and *Salish Weaving*. While there are many more published works which could have been referenced in each section of my paper, for interest of brevity I have limited this essay to a few samples from each of these three discourses as I have identified them. These samples are representational examples of each discourse, but not exhaustive; another writer without my experience as a knitter or my access to archival records kept on Vancouver Island might have chosen other references, and in doing so would have missed making some of the observations in the second section of my paper..

Section 1: Authoritarian and Colonial Writings on Cowichan Woolworking

Published works about Cowichan woolworking evolved from brief and patronizing anthropological notes and comments on traditional blankets, first by explorers and then by Colonial surveyors and authorities, to commentary meant for a general audience on the development of trade in woollen clothing by Cowichan knitters. Throughout these examples of the colonial discourse, agendas of the writers change as time passes; the constant element throughout this discourse is that Cowichan woolworking is foreign to both the writer and the intended audience of readers. While there are distinctions between different colonial writers, this paradigm was evident from 18th-century reports by explorers for European colonial projects, and it continued to appear consistently throughout 20th-century articles by academics and journalists.

When Cook's midshipman George Vancouver led his own journey to the Pacific Northwest in 1792, his journal recorded his meeting with a chief in ceremonial garments; after describing the chief's woollen robe and headdress, Vancouver concluded that "The whole exhibited a magnificent appearance, and indicated a taste for dress and ornament, that we had not supposed the natives of these regions to possess."[4] While Vancouver made meticulous maps of the coastline, he had a dismissive tendency at times to conflate distinct First Nations groups into the vague category of "natives of these regions" – all of whom were foreign to him and to the English lords who read Vancouver's journal.

The botanist for Captain Vancouver, Archibald Menzies, described traditional Coast Salish weaving in his own journal. "We saw them at work on a kind of coarse blanket made of double twisted woollen yarn and curiously wove by their fingers with great patience and ingenuity into various figures," Menzies wrote, quoted by weaver Paula Gustafson in her book *Salish Weaving*. He called the Coast Salish robes "Thick cloth that would baffle the powers of more civilized artists with all their implements to imitate" (31). To his intended readers among the scientific community in Britain, Menzies managed to convey his curiosity and admiration for the "patience and ingenuity" of Coast Salish weavers, even though he did not consider them civilized.

Neither did officials of the Crown Colony of Vancouver Island consider the local indigenous people to be civilized; soon after the colony's founding in 1848, official records record that a British standard of dress had been imposed on local First Nations people instead of a blanket pinned around the shoulders as a robe. Scholar Sylvia Olsen noted that "Colonial government, social reformers, and churches saw knitting and handicrafts as a way to domesticate and 'civilize' indigenous people" (140). Clothing was only one way to impose colonial standards on First Nations people, but it was a very visible imposition, and effort was necessary for people to make clothing or buy it.

As observed by independent scholar Tom Swanky and other commentators, in the aftermath of smallpox epidemics in the 1830s and in 1862 it was important for the surviving members of the Cowichan nation to find new resources for maintaining self-sufficiency: the Colonial officials began to impose a money-oriented economy, and Cowichan fishing and hunting lands were assigned to Colonists by corrupt officials (Swanky 303-304; Twigg 43; and Dorricott and Cullon 152 and 211). One of the reasons for the adoption of knitting by Cowichan people was the changing weather. Garments were needed for warmth as well as to meet the new dress standard, for as Captain Richards' journals observed during his survey of Vancouver Island, from 1858-1862 the weather turned abruptly colder than it had been for many years. Warm garments were necessary and sought after, as blankets were no longer adequate clothing.[5] As well as making clothing for themselves, Cowichan knitters were encouraged by church officials and government Indian Agents to enter the money economy of the new colony by making knitted garments to sell to settlers; knitters and craftsmen were rewarded through cash prizes at public shows that were advertised on posters and in newspapers written for the benefit of literate settlers.

As Olsen reports from her reading of church records, "The first Indian Agricultural and Industrial Show took place in Cowichan in 1869." With the support of the Archdeacon and settlers, 145 lots of Indian samples of produce and manufacture were displayed on tables next to the chief's house by the river: "...Everything from knitting to needlework and baskets to potatoes, pigs, and seed grain was put on display" (Olsen 142). The day concluded with a canoe race between five white men and five Indians, and as many local church-supported events still record in their minutes for parishioners to this day, "a good time was had by all." Local shows of this kind were a display not only of personal pride for each entrant, but of Colonial success, as history scholars have noted: "Exhibitions, from international world fairs to community fall fairs such as the one at Cowichan, stood alongside missionaries as beacons of civilization, boldly proclaiming the economic successes of the colonial project" (Olsen 144). Monetary prizes were offered in each category, and each show was described in great detail in local newspapers on Vancouver Island, and in government reports.[6] By 1880, as Cowichan knitters became familiar with their new skills, there were comments of praise from church and government officials in their official records and quoted in newspapers.

Internationally, knitted goods from Cowichan were displayed at the 1898 World's Fair in Omaha, Nebraska, and also to great acclaim at the 1893 Chicago World's Fair.[7] For decades, international expositions of this kind displayed conflicting messages about First Nations people as foreigners living in a modern world. On some occasions, exhibits displayed First Nations people performing stereotypical pre-Colonial activities, alongside exhibits of people from the same or different First Nations demonstrating their talents at the skills of European civilization such as knitting. Newspapers had field days in which many forgettable articles were written[8], cheerfully praising each fair's fascinating exhibits of human progress.

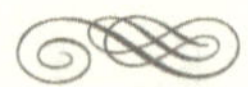

Scholarly Observations

In the early years of the 20th century, C.F. Newcombe was one of several anthropologists to notice that spinning wheels and foot-treadle sewing machines had been re-built by Cowichan men during the 1880s to invent a unique kind of spinning head, driven by a foot-treadle and oriented at a right angle to the European spinning head. These "Indian Spinning Heads" were efficient for producing heavy woollen yarn; they were adopted by many First Nations woolworkers across North America and discussed by anthropologists such as Mary Kissell writing about "peoples of lower culture."[9] Both Kissell and Newcombe wrote from the perspective of Euro-centric anthropologists discussing a foreign culture, for Euro-centric and colonialist academic readers.

Scholarly works which mention Cowichan or Coast Salish woolworking were mostly articles rather than book-length works until after 1950. Up to the theses completed by Brian Thom in 2005 and Sara Perry in 2006, the major academic work of interest on the topic of Cowichan woolworking has been Barbara S. Lane's short book, *The Cowichan Knitting Industry* (1951). While this work is brief, it is detailed and includes several photographs of woolworking tools and wool textiles. Wilson Duff's book *The Indian History of British Columbia* (1964) includes a reference to Lane's work. Both of these works are volumes in the *Anthropology in BC* series released by the Royal British Columbia Provincial Museum. In striving for an academic tone and an anthropological perspective, both Lane and Duff give a twofold impression that seems to be inadvertent: first, that Coast Salish knitters needed to be recorded in history before disappearing as Coast Salish traditional weavers had apparently already done, and second, that these knitted works were simple, unsophisticated, and unremarkable.

Sharply contrasted with Lane's and Duff's works is *Cowichan Indian Knitting* (1987), a short monograph by Margaret Meikle in which Meikle acknowledged her debt to the 1985 oral history project of three Cowichan Band members: Ramona Williams, Eva Williams, and Joyce Underwood. This slim paperback not only has a more informal tone than the scholarly articles in its bibliography, but gives a more human impression of the knitters themselves. By including direct quotations from interview subjects, and candid photographs of woolworkers in their homes with their working materials and their children, Meikle succeeds in putting her human subjects in context with the competitive markets for their knitted goods. The result is a reference which has been more widely read than most scholarly works which mention Cowichan woolworking.

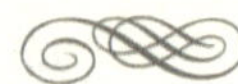

Gradually Increasing Inclusivity

At the beginning of the 1900s, the Red Cross and other organizations began to take notice of the quality and quantity of knitted work produced by First Nations women across Canada. During the First World War, "Indian women... formed patriotic and Red Cross societies on their reserves," wrote Timothy Winegard in *For King and Kanata: Canadian Indians and the First World War*: "The Canadian Red Cross Society stated that articles made by Indian women were the finest quality of knitting and sewing they received" (140). Winegard also noted that the knitted goods sent by Cowichan women as donations for the First World War were considered by the Red Cross to be the finest work seen in Canada for this purpose, as the socks and mittens were thick wool that was warm to wear even when damp.

In Canadian newspapers, articles about Cowichan knitting began to appear at intervals from about 1930 to 1990. There are several samples in the British Columbia Archives, mostly from local newspapers and magazines, often based in Canada's western provinces. The articles are usually local interest stories, in which the reporter marvels that Indian women are making and selling sweaters, hats and work socks. The tone is often cheerful to the point of booster-ism, mostly praise about the sweaters, as if it were a pleasant surprise that Cowichan knitters were able to sell their knitted goods. Photographs, if any, tend to show a knitter standing outdoors with a sweater in her hands, squinting into bright sunshine.

A classic example of these cheery articles is Olive Johnston's 1962 piece for the *Family Herald*, which billed itself as "Canada's Farm Magazine," one of many magazines which specialize in presenting articles about hard-working women. The woman profiled in this article is Jeremina Colvin, who settled at Cowichan Bay in 1885. From the title alone – "Pioneer Woman's Gift to the Cowichans" – readers can see at once the lingering colonialist perspective of this article. Colvin is presented as an admirable woman and a true friend to her Cowichan Indian neighbours: the skill of spinning and knitting in the Fair-Isle style is something that she has given them, so that they were able to make sweaters for their husbands or to sell for $5. This article is not negative or condescending in tone when the Cowichan women are discussed, but it is still patronizing as Johnston eulogizes the late Colvin:

The best memorial to her memory is the fact that descendants of the women she taught are able to give their families a better standard of living through the sale of their sweaters. Today, a specially ordered sweater may bring over $40. It is doubtful, though, if any sweater, no matter how well done, can compare with the last one Jeremina Colvin knit for her son when she was over 80 years of age.[10]

By the 1990s, the tone of these articles had shifted toward the matter-of-fact, as in Jena MacPherson's piece for a travel magazine. To her readers – who are mostly non-Indigenous citizens of the USA and Canada – MacPherson gives plain advice about visiting the Native Heritage Centre in Duncan, BC, and shops which carry sweaters and knitted accessories, just as she would give for travellers to any foreign place. At least this article's photograph of Cowichan women knitting shows them smiling naturally.[11]

When works by West Coast fiction writers began in the 1980s to include novels and stories describing anecdotally what it was like to do the work that many Coast Salish people were doing outdoors during long, rainy winters – such as logging, fishing, digging clams – then fictional characters began to appear who wore warm woollen clothing knitted in Cowichan style. Among the many writers of fiction set on the West Coast are Indigenous authors, authors of colonial descent or born elsewhere in Canada, authors of mixed descent, and new immigrants to Canada and its West Coast.Characters wearing

Cowichan knitting make a few appearances in Canadian fiction, wearing "Siwash sweaters" or "Indian sweaters" in some novels by writers from British Columbia or the Prairie provinces.

With the trend to inclusive mentions of Cowichan knitting, it's no surprise that interest among local print media still remains high; but the colonial discourse is still present in published commentary on Cowichan woolworking, more than 240 years after Cook's 1778 expedition to the Northwest Coast. Though the Colonial perspective that formerly dismissed Cowichan woollen robes as merely the work of uncivilized heathens and not proper clothing has since mellowed to such an interculturally tolerant extent that statements by government officials are no longer patronizing, even a casual reading of recently published articles – whether for academics or the general public – reveals the continuing survival of the old colonial paradigm that this Cowichan cultural practice is foreign to the writer and to the intended readers.

Section 2: Writings by Fibre Arts Specialists on Cowichan Woolworking

In the colonial discourse of published works on Cowichan woolworking, writers saw Cowichan people as foreigners and their works as foreign, a paradigm which perpetuated a Euro-centric view marvelling that the Cowichan were able to make anything at all, let alone anything so well-made as their traditional woven robes, and emphasized that Cowichan people learned the modern techniques of knitting from Europeans. By contrast, the fibre arts writing of the mid-20th century represents a paradigm shift revealing an emerging opinion among some fibre arts scholars and professionals, an opinion which marvelled instead at the interesting variations of knitting style developed by Cowichan knitters. The Cowichan knitters, after all, had changed what they learned of knitting into their own regional style, comparable to other regional styles around the world, such as damask, intarsia, argyle, Aran, Greek, Afghani or others. In the fibre arts discourse, writers did continue to recognize the Cowichan work as foreign, but this foreign nature was considered simply as one kind of foreignness among many diverse kinds, each of which was being recognized for its own qualities. The intended readers might be knitters of any tradition, or students of the fibre arts more broadly, not only people of the same traditions as the writer. The change from a colonialist perspective to a fibre arts perspective in what was written did not happen all at one moment in time for all writers; the change in what was written proceeded gradually during the latter half of the 20th century for individual fibre arts writers as they compared and contrasted regional styles of fibre arts.

Many of these types of sources recognize that textiles from around the world can have variations of cultural significance as well as their mundane purposes, and speak approvingly of regional variations.[12] At one point in her encyclopaedic history of knitting, Lela Nargi refers to Barbara Walker's knitting patterns based on fragments recovered from the Roman fort Dura-Europos, dated to 300 BCE, and located in present-day Syria on the high banks of the Euphrates River. Walker wrote: "*Knitter, let your hands reach back twenty centuries into the past and touch the hands of your unknown cultural ancestor who made that ancient fragment...*" (14). Knitters from other cultures have stated their solidarity with international knitters who incorporate their own traditional elements in their work.[14]

By the end of the twentieth century, books by fibre artists discussed both traditional Coast Salish weaving and modern Cowichan knitting in the same terms and with the same respect as they discussed the fibre arts of any part of the world. Until 2007, there were few easily available scholarly works on Indigenous knitting, and even fewer which cited books from knitting publishers. Instead, the act of citation usually was done by the writers of fibre arts books: Priscilla Gibson-Roberts and

Paula Gustafson, for example, each cited Margaret Meikle's monograph. Any book published since 2000 which is intended to describe a variety of international styles of knitting includes a reference to Cowichan knitting, at least a brief mention of it as the only indigenous folk knitting in North America. Nargi's book in particular has a chapter on Cowichan Indian knitting which describes this knitting style in the same terms and with the same sense of community and admiration as do the chapters for regional styles from countries as varied as Turkey, Peru, or Japan.

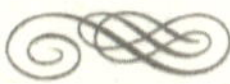

Origin of the Cowichan Sweater

Nowhere in published commentaries on Cowichan woolworking is the paradigm shift from the colonial discourse to the fibre arts discourse more apparent than in discussions of the origin of the Cowichan Indian sweater, and nowhere is it more clear that this paradigm shift was not a general cultural shift common to all writers of that time but instead a change among only some of the fibre arts scholars and professionals. In a distinct change from the regional newspaper and magazine articles mentioned in section 1, publisher Sue Hodgson was able to print in a locally distributed magazine on the arts in Victoria her July 2012 interview about a recent award-winning book on the vibrant fibre work of Coast Salish artists, in which Hodgson made inclusive observations rather than colonialist ones:

> *Cowichan sweaters were, in the first place, a wonderful fusion of traditional Coast Salish blanket making skills and techniques and European (especially Scottish)*

> *knitting practices and tools (knitting needles). It is the woolworking in both peoples that has deep roots and important cultural significance. Ingenuity and need created the specific products.*[14]

The unique Cowichan or Indian sweater was not a one-time inspired invention by a single knitter, but was developed in a series of changes between about 1870 and 1910, and the changes were shared among nearby Coast Salish groups. Sylvia Olsen calls this style of sweater "a cultural fusion yet at the same time a truly native innovation" (147). She and other writers have reported that the first plain sweaters, one-colour ganseys, were made in Cowichan when the Sisters of Saint Ann taught knitting in their school, which opened in 1864. A gansey or guernsey is a distinct style of working man's sweater knit on the eponymous island of Guernsey in Great Britain. Between 1900 and 1910 Cowichan sweaters changed to have bands of two-colour patterning and unique shawl collars, features of what is considered classic "Cowichan" style (though the style is practised by many Coast Salish groups). Olsen makes a good case for a Coast Salish woman of the Songhees band in Victoria knitting the first of these sweaters in 1906, when the woman's son complained about the itchy feel of commercial woollen undershirts; Olsen adds that relatives spread the sweater concept to Cowichan.

However, at least one part of this origin story can be contradicted: my close study of the archives of the Sisters of Saint Anne has revealed that there were no sweater patterns taught at their schools in Victoria (founded 1858 when the Sisters came from their home convent in Vaudreuil, Quebec) or Cowichan (founded 1864), and none are recorded in the knitting journal handwritten in French by Sister Mary Stanislas Kosca from 1866 to 1880, during her time at the sisters' school in Cowichan. The nuns' patterns included socks and mittens in the first few years, then long woollen underwear and toques (knitted hats) by 1870, and only one example of two-colour work at the end of Kosca's journal, a striped baby hat using one colour of yarn per row.

I cannot consult Cowichan patterns in this matter, as there are no knitting patterns from 1870 to 1910 preserved by Cowichan knitters; and indeed, until the mid-twentieth century, knitting patterns were not used among Cowichan knitters, few of whom could read or write English, as Olsen and Gibson-Roberts have noted. A few knitters drew on graph paper to mark out the large images they designed for the midsection of sweaters, but they did not use complete knitting patterns as such.

In newspaper articles about Cowichan knitting and Coast Salish knitting, as quoted earlier in this essay, the theory is often reiterated that settler Jeremina Colvin taught her Indian friends how to make the Cowichan sweater in Fair-Isle style. The source was her son Magnus Colvin, who claimed repeatedly in interviews after Jeremina's death that the origin of the Cowichan sweater was when his mother taught Fair-Isle knitting to Cowichan people. As a founding member of the association Native Sons of Cowichan (the local branch of the Native Sons of British Columbia, an all-white group of settler's sons, named with no sense of irony), he had a vested interest in representing his family as belonging in the Cowichan area, and being well-integrated with their neighbours. Previously published interviews with Magnus Colvin were the source for most later articles and books which stated that Cowichan sweaters were derivative of Fair-Isle sweaters. The British Columbia Archives holds at least 31 newspaper articles dated from 1940 to 1990 repeating and rephrasing the same "Colvin origin theory" in stories about Cowichan knitting, even when the journalist is writing about other Coast Salish groups such as the Tsartlip and Clallum bands. From newspaper articles, this misapprehension has made its way into some of the knitting literature.

But it is clear to fabric arts scholar Lela Nargi that the "Colvin origin theory" is an overly simplistic relationship drawn between Cowichan and Fair-Isle sweaters; Cowichan sweaters were not made after Fair-Isle sweaters and based on their techniques, because in fact Cowichan sweaters were already undergoing the changes to their modern form when Fair-Isle sweaters were first made for sale in 1910 (Nargi 53). Jeremina Colvin emigrated from the Shetland Islands to Cowichan in 1885, before any documentation exists to show that the two-colour-a-row technique was present in the Shetlands. Colvin could have learned Fair-Isle two-colour knitting from letters and from other settlers, and it is certain that she did teach spinning and knitting to her friends among Cowichan women, but the sweaters Jeremina Colvin made at first were turtleneck pullovers in one colour, and it was not until later in her life that she made Fair-Isle sweaters.

Nargi also observes that Fair-Isle knitting is usually done in fine two-ply or three-ply yarns with a moderate tension on the needles. Yarn in Cowichan sweaters is traditionally a soft, bulky, handspun single strand, or in recent decades has been a machine-spun six-ply with minimal twist which produces similar bulk; in either case, the yarn is knitted with tight tension on needles that are more slender than a European knitter would use for such bulky yarn. The result is that a Cowichan sweater is a much firmer, denser, heavier, and longer-lasting garment than a Fair-Isle sweater. A Cowichan sweater is guaranteed to last through thirty years of hard use (Gibson-Roberts and Robson 185).

The colonialist story in which Colvin taught Cowichan knitters how to make their iconic sweater is also contradicted by evidence from archival photographs and from knitting histories. When Colvin arrived in Cowichan, Coast Salish woolworkers were already experimenting with ways to use elements of their traditional weaving to create fitted garments for the upper body. Photographs from between 1890 and 1919 exist in the British Columbia Archives showing jackets made from cut and sewn pieces of traditional Coast Salish blankets. As the 19th century ended, woolworkers were already experimenting with warm, fitted garments of their own design incorporating twine and twill weave, and constructed like a European jacket or heavy sweater with set-in sleeves.

The "Colvin origin theory" is also contradicted by knitting histories based on consultations with Cowichan knitters, such as those written by fibre arts professional Priscilla Gibson-Roberts; Gibson-Roberts has conducted many interviews with Coast Salish knitters around the Pacific Northwest. *"Oral tradition offers an alternate story,"* she wrote in *Knitting in the Old Way*, *"that a group of Cowichan women traded for a British fisherman's gansey, which they studied to determine the construction techniques necessary for making a sweater"* (184). Among Cowichan knitters, their oral tradition is that while on Valdez Island in the 1890s, knitters traded to get a sweater from a British sailor, and unravelled it to figure out how it was made. Gibson-Roberts was the first writer to put in print this oral tradition. This act of reverse-engineering is an indication that the Cowichan knitters had a sophisticated understanding of knitting technology, rather than the simpler practise of merely following directions. If we allow the textiles to speak for themselves, too, the construction of a Cowichan sweater reveals that it is based on gansey structure, not Fair-Isle sweater structure; this observation supports the oral tradition rather than the "Colvin origin" theory.

While Colvin did knit and spin with her friends, including her friends among Cowichan knitters, and may have taught them two-colour work, the unique style of the Cowichan sweater has some different elements from Fair-Isle work, including twined stitching; this twined stitching leads me into speculation about a possible Swedish or Scandinavian influence on the two-colour work and patterning. A quality of the Cowichan Sweater construction that is apparent on close inspection is that the two-colour-a-row patterning is not knitted in Fair-Isle style, which would carry the unused colour of yarn loosely across the back of the work. Instead, in a Cowichan Sweater, the two strands of yarn are twisted at every stitch, leaving no loose loops of yarn on the inside of the sweater to catch and pull. By twisting the two strands at every stitch, Cowichan knitters are using a style which also is used in Sweden.

For four reasons, I suggest that it is possible that Cowichan knitters might have traded for and unravelled a piece of Scandinavian knitting as well as a gansey. First, I would propose that this twined knitting style is reminiscent of the twined weaving in traditional Coast Salish blankets, which could suggest that the Cowichan knitters who began twisting the two strands of yarn after every stitch in their two-colour rows were trying to make a style of knitting which twisted the yarn at every stitch in order to be like the twined weaving in their traditional blankets. Second, this two-colour work twined after every stitch in Cowichan Indian sweaters is much like Swedish *tvåändssticknìng* (twined knitting), which is used to make sturdy mitts and hats (Gibson-Roberts and Robson 230). Third, there were Norwegians and Swedes not only among the colonial settlers in the 1870s and 1880s, but even a century earlier as workers living on the coast in Russian fur-trading centres in Sitka and other locations in what is now Alaska. Fourth and lastly, throughout the 19th century it was common for Scandinavian sweaters to have bands of two-colour decorations around wrists and waist or shoulders, unlike Fair-Isle sweaters which were not made until the beginning of the 20th century and which tended to stack several bands of two-colour decorations around the body and sleeves. No writer has commented in print, so far as I have been able to determine, on whether this twined strand style of colour work in Cowichan Sweaters could be a possible sign of Scandinavian influence, or on whether the twined strand knitting is a conscious analogue of twined weaving.

Ultimately, the Cowichan Indian sweater is described by fibre arts scholars not as an example of Fair-Isle knitting, but as a unique invention born of cultural fusion, starting with gansey structure, knitted in a two-colour-a-row style, and using decorative knitted designs of three kinds: a few traditional from Cowichan weaving and basket-making, several Fair-Isle, and many newly devised, in particular the large images on the main body of some sweaters. What may not be apparent to academic scholars is that when artists and artisans of any nation or culture meet each other, as Olsen notes, it is common for them to observe each other's style of art or craft and to permit each other to practise those elements of it which are not considered proprietary or secret; this practise is akin to "jamming" among musicians, and is similarly not intended to be nor is it considered the equivalent of theft or plagiarism or appropriation, at least, as long as the learner does not claim to be producing authentic work of the other culture. *"Of course, no one asked the indigenous artists and craftspeople, who were just doing what artists always do – learning new techniques and incorporating them into the old – what was authentic,"* wrote Olsen. She went on to add: *"If, as cultural commentator Marshall McLuhan said, 'the artist is the person who invents the means to bridge between biological inheritance and the environments created by technological innovation,' then the early Coast Salish knitters were truly artists and Cowichan sweaters a fine example of his viewpoint"* (177). Fibre arts professionals in particular, from many cultures, consider it appropriate to learn about other styles of fibre art and to acknowledge their sources and influences; significantly, there are no copyrights in Western nations for fashion design, though trademarks for designer labels are recognized.

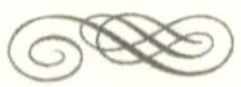

Cowichan Influence on European-style Knitting

The invention of the "Cowichan sweater" around 1900-1910 was the development of a unique style of sweater as a new form of work clothing and consumer good, which was at first of local interest only. As "Cowichan sweaters" or "Indian sweaters" were regularly worn by a great many famous people from the 1930s to the 1990s, this style of knitting was discussed favourably in magazines and books by knitting publishers. Whether these professionals were marketing crafts materials nationally, writing popular books and craft magazines, or writing about fine arts, these fibre arts professionals did not treat Cowichan woolworking as if it were a marginal or dying art, or only of anthropological interest. Instead, they treated Cowichan and Coast Salish knitting as a living art, and one of the many international and admirable styles of knitting. Writing for an international audience of readers from many nations, commentators discussed Cowichan knitting on a par with styles from other parts of the world. Entrepreneurs discussed how to emulate it, without all that tedious hand-spinning or knitting heavy yarn at a tight tension.

The distinctive appearance of Cowichan Indian style knitting made lasting impressions, not only on the people wearing the garments, but on the hand knitting industry. One of the designers influenced by Cowichan and Coast Salish fibre artists was Regine Faust (née Schuett), a German fashion designer and magazine writer who in 1939 became the first woman granted a Master's degree by the Knitting Guild in Germany. "Regine's design principles are already clearly visible in a hand knit matching mother and daughter sweater set produced in 1940," noted Canadian art historian Ann Davis. "Here, stylized two dimensional animals are contained in horizontal bands" (Davis n.p.). While it was not uncommon in the 20th century for Germans to be fascinated with the little they could learn of North American First Nations cultures, Faust did not make copies of fake "Indian" art; instead, Faust integrated the motifs she studied into her own designs for knitted garments and accessories, and made note of her sources.[15] The result was that she made strikingly original books of patterns for hand knitting with needles or small knitting machines the size of an electronic keyboard, which she used as a teacher at an Ontario college.

At the same time as Faust arrived in Ontario, Willard and Olive McPhedrain moved their family woollen mill business to Ontario from Sifton, Manitoba. *"In the 1950's, no other company had its finger more firmly on the pulse of the Canadian knitter than Mary Maxim!"* boasts the website for the Mary Maxim Company, which is *"the largest mail order merchandiser of exclusive needlework and craft kits in North America."* Expanding the family business from work socks and woollen blankets into the market for hand knitting in 1954, McPhedrain renamed it after a family employee, Mary Maximchuk, a knitter of mixed descent. Inspired by the motifs of Cowichan Indian knitting, McPhedrain put his designers to work creating graphs for knitting patterns. Among other needlework and craft kits, to this day the company sells patterns and kits to make what their website calls *"bulky outdoor zippered jackets to knit using the first easy-to-follow graph-style charts."* The Mary Maxim approach is to make simple sweaters with raglan sleeves, working in commercial yarns of acrylic fibres. The first decorative designs on these sweater/jackets were imitations of Cowichan motifs, which are still available sixty years later. The designers quickly began their practice of creating designs based on hockey team jerseys, and moved on to design motifs allowing knitters to make jackets with sports team logos, John Deere tractors, Cookie Monster, and other identifiable representational images.

An important observation to make at this point is that between 1850 and 1940, except for Cowichan knitting there was no knitting style in Europe and North America which used representational images in decorative designs; for knitters in most parts of the world, both colour work – often an imitation of intricate Persian hand-knotted carpets or damask weaving – and texture work were so stylized that decorative designs had become abstracted of meaning. For example, only a handful of Scandinavian and Fair-Isle designs are recognizable as flowers or snowflakes. An element of Cowichan knitting that has had international influence was the invention of motifs that can be recognized as animals, people, or objects. The idea for representational images as knitting motifs is an element of Cowichan knitting that is most easily adopted by other knitting styles. The result of this syzygy of knitting styles is that there are many Cowichan-inspired sweaters being hand-made by knitters who have never seen and handled these heavy woollen garments with set-in sleeves. The direction of influence no longer proceeds only from Europe through French-Canadian nuns and Scots colonists to First Nations woolworkers; the Coast Salish knitters have had a profound influence on knitting trends around the world through their own works and the derivative works of Faust, Mary Maxim and other companies' designs.[16]

Section 3: The Indigenous Artists' Perspective

A discerning reader could ask at this point: what is the perspective of the Cowichan woolworker about her or his own work, and about cultural appropriation by non-indigenous people or foreigners? It's better to ask what are the perspectives of indigenous artists; the plural form of this question is definitely necessary, as there are many contributors to this cultural art form, some of whom practise related creative disciplines, some of whom are from other Coast Salish groups, and some who through years of study, teaching, and curatorial experience have become recognized as scholars of the arts of other First Nations as well as their own indigenous heritage. Among artists with such a diverse range of experience it is natural that perspectives will vary, and that only some of these perspectives will appear in print; the published opinions of some artists will be discussed here.

Tom Hill of Six Nations is one of these artists and scholars with curatorial experience who has commented directly upon the question of whether foreign fibre arts professionals are necessarily colonial imperialists who are appropriating indigenous arts. As well, at least one European fibre arts professional is treated as a colleague by Hill. In his introduction to the 1980 re-release of Regine Faust's book *American Indian Designs Adapted to Knitting*, Hill calls Faust's *"work a synthesis of all the influences, European and Amerindian cultures, art and technology. Her distinctive approach should prove to be a welcome inspiration to knit designers from all cultural backgrounds."*[17] Hill's statement shows that he considers Faust to be a fellow artist who acknowledges her sources and influences; significantly, Hill is not issuing blanket approval of all European artists producing works derivative of First Nations designs, just his approval of Faust's synthesis and distinctive approach of citing her sources. It's important to note as well that Hill cannot be considered the sole authority who speaks for all First Nations artists, though in the terms of the present project, his work is usefully representative.

In what I have identified as the indigenous discourse of the published works on Cowichan woolworking, the woolworkers do not simply present a mirror image of the colonial dichotomy of Self and Other; the woolworkers are speaking from the viewpoint of people who make and wear these fabrics, and for them the Others are not so much non-Salish as people who need an explanation. Unlike the colonial discourse, in which writers speak to readers like themselves about the foreign, in the indigenous discourse writers are speaking about the fabrics they make and use, and the people they are addressing are those who need an explanation: mostly foreigners, though also students and indigenous youth.

Hill is not the only indigenous artist who can find him/herself being treated by journalists and academics as an ambassador, a translator, a teacher, or someone who has to make explanations to foreigners. *"Because of the visibility of the artist's work, he or she may unwittingly become a spokesperson for the community, tribe, or native people as a whole,"* wrote curator Barbara Brotherton in the introduction to a book based on a show she curated of Coast Salish artworks (4). As Brotherton observed, Coast Salish artist Qualsius Shaun Peterson uses a metaphor of paddling his canoe, as part of a team pulling their paddle strokes together in perfect alignment, when Peterson advocates for pulling one's life and art together with a single focus. Speaking on Coast Salish weaving in particular, it *"is really part of a larger whole that can't be extracted,"* as artist Debra Sparrow said in *S'abadeb – The Gifts. "If you extract it, you take it out of its context, and you lose some of its power and its meaning"* (245).

Before the arrival of the explorers and colonial peoples, none of the First Nations in the Pacific Northwest seem to have had a traditional written literature; the First Nations used other ways to communicate their cultures, histories and stories to themselves and each other, and for the Coast Salish people, one of their ways was through the use of their traditional weaving. During the 1700s and 1800s, European and Russian visitors to the Pacific Northwest Coast of what is now British Columbia commented upon the blankets woven and worn by the First Nations peoples. Woollen blankets or robes were mentioned, as well as robes woven of beaten cedar bark. These textiles performed some of the same functions that written texts do: these textiles were carefully made, culturally significant objects that could be used by one person to communicate with others. Coast Salish weaving in general and the making of ceremonial regalia in particular was controlled by cultural norms, reminiscent in some ways to how Canadians now regulate copyright, patents, identification cards, and oaths of office. Some of these cultural norms were considered private or secret, and none of them were respected by the Canadian government for over a hundred years, so it is an inclusive experience to read recent works on woolworking being written in English by Coast Salish artists and intended for general readers.

While a survey could be done sensitively of dozens of Cowichan fibre artists and return dozens of different individual opinions about their collective art, as well as about work by non-indigenous artists that is influenced by Cowichan work, this paper *Woolgathering* is a brief study instead, primarily about textual representations rather than the woolworking itself, and accordingly it has worked from already published texts, studying the opinions expressed there. The opinions of many Coast Salish fibre artists are quoted throughout the book *Working With Wool* by Sylvia Olsen and the National Film Board documentary *The Story of the Coast Salish Knitters* by Metis film-maker Mary Welsh. As well, there are artists' statements in the books *Time Warp: Contemporary Textiles of the Northwest Coast, Transporters I LECILEN,* and *S'abadeb – The Gifts*, which accompanied the multi-media art shows of the same names. Coast Salish fabric artists Debra Sparrow and her sister Robyn Sparrow, whose works appeared in the *Time Warp* show, are not alone in their stories of learning from old fabrics kept in museums as well as from contemporary fabric artists.

A common trope of these works is experiences the Coast Salish artists had and continue to have when selling their works. Some of the knitters profiled in Welsh's film speak candidly of how their interest in exploring new knitting techniques is sometimes frustrated by marketing's preference for "authentic"

Cowichan knitting; the store managers that retail their knitted garments won't accept experimental variations of colours or textures, because the managers believe customers insist on "traditional" Cowichan knitting. Later in the film, another knitter describes her resolution to sell her knitted goods directly to her customers, rather than through a store. Olsen's book details the frustrations endured by her mother-in-law and neighbours when selling sweaters to stores; the Olsens founded a small business that retailed sweaters on-reserve instead of in downtown Victoria, and this business continues to thrive under the grandchildren's management.

Bridging gaps between media is another trope found in published works made in close consultation with Cowichan and Coast Salish artists, for the fibre artists often explain in artists' statements that they are commonly working in more than one medium, or in co-operation with artists working in another form; relatives or associates might explore culturally or visually similar work in fibre arts, basket-making, wood carving, or painting. For the art shows *Time Warp* and *S'abadeb – The Gifts* and books based on these shows, woolworks are often displayed with paintings, baskets, and carvings, and curatorial notes emphasize how these diverse works have elements in common.

In one of the articles in *Transporters I LECILEN* there is a crucial element of cultural fusion in a description of John Marston's carving "*'ehhwe'p syuth* (To Share History)." Editor Andrea Walsh co-wrote an article observing that after Marston visited Papua New Guinea, he integrated his own traditional Coast Salish carving style with what he had learned during a four-week artistic exchange with Sepik River master carvers. *"Marston very deliberately carved one side of the dramatic sculpture as he would have before his time in the Sepik,"* noted Walsh, *"and the other with an openness to the growth and influence he experienced in these remote tribal communities"* (33). As an artist who avoids formulaic work, Marston was committed to recognizing the influences of that completely new environment. Among several multi-media shows of modern Coast Salish art, Marston's work is far from unique in its elements of cultural fusion, because many fibre art pieces are displayed with artists' statements which describe cross-cultural influences.

While it is possible to consider Marston's – and his colleagues' – incorporation of cultural fusion to be a modern divergence from traditional First Nations cultural norms, there is textile evidence that cultural fusion in the fibre arts has a long history on the Northwest Coast. In her discussions of technical transitions among four styles of traditional weaving on the Northwest Coast (Coast Salish, Raven's Tail, Cedar Bark, and Chilkat), weaver Cheryl Samuel discusses the many robes collected in 1778 by James Cook. Though these robes were collected in one place, at Nootka among the Nuu-chah-nulth people, only two of the robes Cook collected were made at or near that place. The people at Nootka had traded among people of other cultures to acquire the other diverse robes; the trading journeys would have been up to a thousand miles along perilous shorelines, a fact which speaks of the value of cultural interactions among First Nations groups before Colonial influence began. One of these robes in particular is now in the *Museum für Völkerkunde* in Vienna, where Samuel inspected it closely; her analysis shows that from the top border to the bottom border, the Vienna Robe is an example of cultural transition. By the time its weaver completed the Vienna Robe, this weaver's techniques changed (Samuel 157). Samuel finds it exciting to speculate about whether the weaver of the Vienna Robe was a leader in the transformation of one form of weaving to another, or whether this weaver was gathering knowledge from the weavings of other tribes. Considered along with other elements of transition among the robes collected by Cook, the Vienna Robe in particular is evidence that for traditional Cowichan weavers and weavers of other First Nations of the Pacific Northwest Coast, fibre arts were not static examples of isolationist cultural practises; on the contrary, there were traditional weavers who (like many contemporary Cowichan and Coast Salish woolworkers) considered their works to be mobile and subject as well to change and influence in many ways to suit the interests of the artists and users and to make good use of the materials available, just as modern Cowichan woolworks continue to be. The discourse of "foreignness," quite simply, is misplaced in discussions of Cowichan woolworking.

Conclusion

As a knitter and storyteller, I find it fascinating to trace these divergent discourses in the commentary on foreignness in published works about Cowichan woolworking, starting with brief, Eurocentric notes by explorers such as Cook and Vancouver writing to their investors and Menzies writing to men of science, then reports made by Colonial authorities, as if they were commenting on quaint anthropological specimens that should soon be replaced by modern improvements. As Cowichan sweaters, socks, mitts, and hats were worn by an increasing number of people from 1900 to the present day, this style of knitting was discussed patronizingly, though often favourably as well, in mass-market newspapers, but always favourably and inclusively in books and magazines about fibre arts. There have been few scholarly works on Cowichan woolworking, but books by fibre arts professionals discuss traditional Coast Salish weaving and modern Coast Salish knitting with the same interest and delight that are seen in discussions of the fibre arts of any nation. In 21st-century works released by or in close consultation with First Nations people, the woolworkers are stating their own thoughts, and for them the foreigner is someone who observes the fabrics instead of making and using them. This definition of foreign is subtly yet profoundly different from that held by the Colonial explorers.

Though it is no more appropriate to assign meaning to a knitted work by a Cowichan woolworker than it would be for Cook or Vancouver to interpret the traditional blankets they saw being used as ceremonial garb, there is an observation that is fair comment to make about these woolworks in general. As Gustafson notes, in pre-Colonial times, Coast Salish ceremonial blankets were woven by the social elite and used for their people of highest status. By contrast, as Olsen observes, Cowichan knitted works are knitted by people of any social standing, and worn by their own family members or sold. Instead of a few women clothing a few of their people for ritual events that took place over thousands of years, since 1900 there are now many women (and some men) clothing people for work and ordinary days – and the people they are clothing are both their own families and people among descendants of the Colonials who choose to wear these garments. The woolworkers continue creating iconic woolworks that are valued by their own people and others, without the support of "dragon" investors from reality television shows. These garments, recognizable at a glance, identify both makers and wearers as people living in close association with this place and time.

Bibliography

Anderson, Nancy Marguerite. "A second view of Anderson's 1847 expedition from Kamloops to Fort Langley." *Fur Trade Family History*. Web. *http://furtradefamilyhistory.blogspot.ca/2012/05/second-view-of-andersons-1847.html* Posted May 20, 2012. Retrieved October 6, 2012.

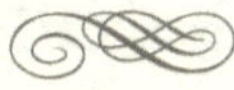

Brotherton, Barbara. *S'abadeb – The Gifts: Pacific Coast Salish Art and Artists*. Vancouver, BC: Douglas & McIntyre, 2008.

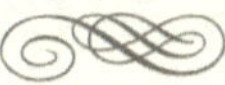

Cook, James. *The Voyages of Captain Cook*, Vol. 2. London, UK: William Smith, 1842.

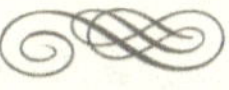

Davis, Ann. "Form & Intuition: Regine Faust's Design." *The Velvet Highway*, Vol. 2 #1, Winter 2006. Web. Retrieved February 6, 2013. http://www.velvethighway.com/RFpages/finding_regine.html

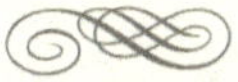

Davis, Chuck. "Sunspots." *The History of Metropolitan Vancouver.* Web. http://www.vancouverhistory.ca/sunspots_jan.htm Posted 2004-2011. Retrieved October 6, 2012.

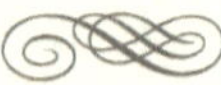

Dorricott, Linda and Deidre Cullon, ed. *The Private Journal of Captain G. H. Richards: The Vancouver Island Survey (1860-1862).* Vancouver, BC: Ronsdale Press, 2012.

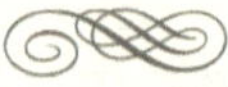

Down, Edith E. *A Century of Service, 1858-1958: A history of the Sisters of Saint Ann and their contribution to education in British Columbia, the Yukon, and Alaska.* Victoria, BC: Sisters of Saint Anne, 1999.

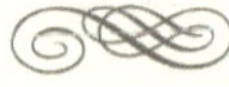

Duff, Wilson. *The Indian History of British Columbia, Vol. 1, Anthropology in BC Memoir #5.* Victoria, BC: Province of British Columbia Department of Recreation and Conservation, 1964.

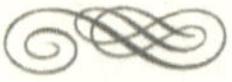

Eells, Myron (1976). *Myron Eells and the Puget Sound Indians.* ed. by Robert H. Ruby and John A. Brown. Seattle: Superior Publishing Co.

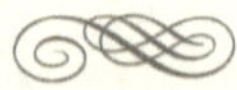

Environment Canada. "Canadian Climate Normals 1971-2012." *National Climate Data and Information Archive*. Fredericton, NB: Environment Canada. Posted May 29, 2012. Retrieved October 6, 2012. http://climate.weatheroffice.gc.ca/climate_normals/results_e.html?stnID=889&lang=e&dCode=1&StationName=VANC

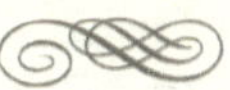

Faust, Regine. *American Indian Designs Adapted to Knitting*. Toronto, ON: Regine Studio, 1980.

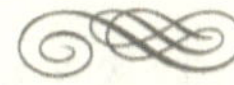

Germaine, Eudice. "Letters/Response to Visual Sermons and Woven Image: Contemporary British Tapestry." *Shuttle Spindle & Dyepot*, Vol. XXVIII No. 2 Spring 1987, p5.

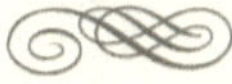

Gibson-Roberts, Priscilla, and Deborah Robson. *Knitting in the Old Way: Designs & Techniques from Ethnic Sweaters*, expanded edition. Fort Collins, CO: Nomad Press, 2004.

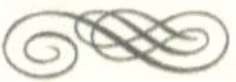

Gibson-Roberts, Priscilla. *Salish Indian Sweaters*. Cambridge, MN: Adventure Publications, 1989.

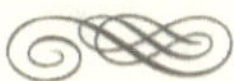

Gough, Barry. *The Northwest Coast: British Navigation, Trade, and Discoveries to 1812*. Vancouver, BC: UBC Press, 1992.

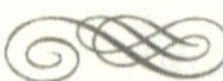

Gustafson, Paula. *Salish Weaving*. Vancouver, BC: Douglas & MacIntyre Ltd, and Seattle, WA: University of Washington Press, 1980.

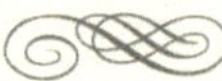

Hill, Tom. "Introduction." *American Indian Designs Adapted To Knitting*, by Regine Faust. Toronto, ON: Regine Studio, 1980.

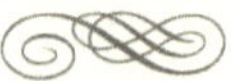

Hodgson, Sue. "Can We Talk? Sylvia Olsen, Author, Designer, On-Reserve Housing Technician." *Seaside Times: Your West Coast Culture*, July 2012. Sidney, BC: Rhino Print Solutions, pp 10-11.

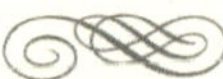

Holm, Bill and Bill Reid. *Indian Art of the Northwest Coast: a Dialogue on Craftsmanship and Aesthetics*. Seattle, WA: University of Washington, 1978.

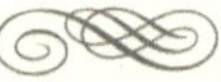

Huck, Barbara. "The Hair of the Dog." *Beaver* April/May 2007, Vol. 87, No. 2, pp 42-44.

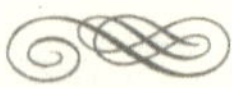

Humphrey, Elaine. "First Nations Wool Dog." *Natural History Presentation*. Natural History Society of Victoria. University of Victoria, Victoria, BC. October 9, 2012. Lecture.

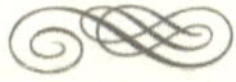

Johnston, Olive L. "Pioneer Woman's Gift to the Cowichans." *Family Herald: Canada's Farm Magazine*, No. 6 February 6, 1962, p34.

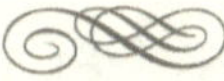

Kissell, Mary Lois. "A New Type of Spinning in North America." *American Anthropologist*, Vol. 18, pp264-270.

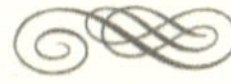

Kosca, Sister Mary Stanislas. *S 29 – 537*. Unpublished notebook. Victoria, BC: Sisters of Saint Anne Archives, ca. 1866-1880.

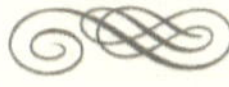

Lamb, William Kaye. "The Mystery of Mrs. Barkley's Diary. Notes on the Voyage of the 'Imperial Eagle,' 1786-87." *British Columbia Historical Quarterly* #6. Victoria: Archives of B.C. And B.C. Historical Association, 1942.

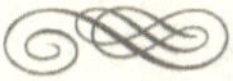

Lane, Barbara (1951). *The Cowichan Knitting Industry. Anthropology in British Columbia, #2*. Victoria: British Columbia Provincial Museum, 1951.

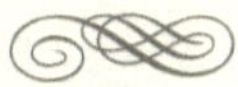

Lewis, Joe. "Finding Regine." *The Velvet Highway*, Vol 1 # 3, Fall 2005. Web. Retrieved February 6, 2013. http://www.velvethighway.com/RFpages/finding_regine.html

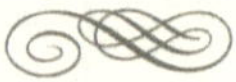

Mackie, Quentin. "Archaeology Theses." *Northwest Coast Archaeology*. Web. http://qmackie.wordpress.com/northwest-archaeology-theses/ Retrieved October 20, 2012.

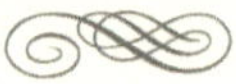

Marr, Carolyn J. *A History of Salish Weaving: The Effects of Culture Change on Textile Tradition*. Unpublished M.A. Thesis. Denver, CO: University of Denver, 1979.

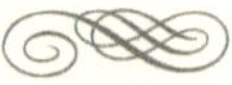

MacPherson, Jena. "Cowichan Sweaters." *Sunset magazine*, Fall 1996. Seattle, WA: Pacific Northwest Travel Guide.

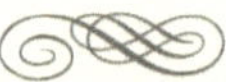

Meikle, Margaret. *Cowichan Indian Knitting*. Vancouver, BC: University of British Columbia Museum of Anthropology, 1987.

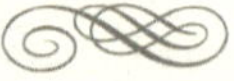

Mary Maxim. "About Mary Maxim." *Mary Maxim Inc.* Web. Retrieved September 24, 2012. http://www.marymaxim.ca/about-marymaxim

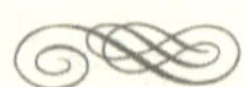

Nargi, Lela. *Knitting Around The World: A Multistranded History of a Time-Honored Tradition.* Minneapolis, MN: Voyageur Press, 2011.

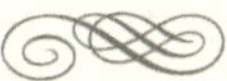

Obama, Michelle. "Remarks by the First Lady at the ribbon cutting ceremony for the Metropolitan Museum." *The White House.* Web. Posted May 18, 2009. Retrieved November 15, 2012. http://www.whitehouse.gov/the-press-office/remarks-first-lady-ribbon-cutting-ceremony-metropolitan-museum-art-american-wing

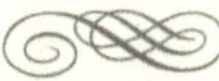

Olsen, Sylvia. *Working With Wool: A Coast Salish legacy & the Cowichan Sweater.* Winlaw, BC: Sono Nis, 2010.

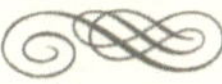

———. *Yetsa's Sweater.* Winlaw, BC: Sono Nis, 2006.

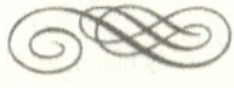

Perry, Sara Elisabeth. *Picturing Prehistory Within (And Without) Science: De-constructing Archaeological Portrayals of the Peopling of New Territories.* Victoria, BC: University of Victoria, 2006.

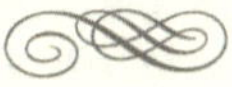

Runkle, Dita. "Cheryl Samuel: Chilkat and Ravenstail Weavings." *Shuttle Spindle & Dyepot,* Vol. XXXI No. 2 Spring 2000, p33-36.

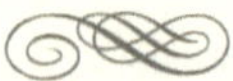

"Salish Fusion Knitworks Pitch." *Dragon's Den*, CBC TV, January 13, 2013. http://www.cbc.ca/dragonsden/2013/01/salish-fusion-knitwear.html

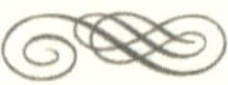

Samuel, Cheryl. *The Raven's Tail.* Vancouver, BC: University of British Columbia Press, 1987. Victoria, BC: Black Crow Books, 2011.

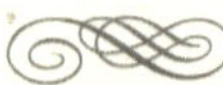

Swanky, Tom. *The True Story Of Canada's "War" Of Extermination On the Pacific plus The Tsilhqot'in and other First Nations Resistance.* Burnaby, BC: Dragon Heart Enterprises, 2012.

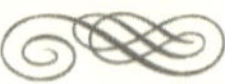

Thom, Brian David. *Coast Salish Senses of Place: Dwelling, Meaning, Power, Property and Territory in the Coast Salish World.* PhD thesis. Montreal, QC: McGill University, 2005.

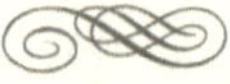

Turner, Nancy J. And Richard J. Hebda. *Saanich Ethnobotany: Culturally Important Plants of the WSANEC People.* Victoria, BC: Royal BC Museum, 2012.

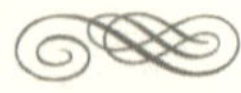

Twigg, Alan. *Aboriginality: The Literary Origins of British Columbia*, Volume 2. Vancouver, BC: Ronsdale Press, 2005.

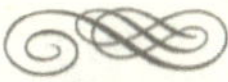

———. *First Invaders: The Literary Origins of British Columbia*, Volume 2. Vancouver, BC: Ronsdale Press, 2004.

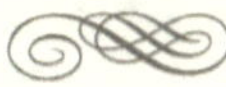

Vancouver, George. *Voyage of Discovery to the North Pacific Oceans and Round the World, 1791-1795*, edited by W.K. Lamb. London, UK: Hakluyt Society, 1984.

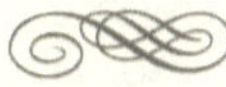

Vanderhoop, Evelyn and Martine Jeanne Reid. *Time Warp: Contemporary Textiles of the Northwest Coast*. Vancouver, BC: Bill Reid Gallery of Northwest Coast Art, 2010.

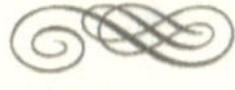

Walker, Barbara. *A Second Treasury of Knitting Patterns*. New York, NY: Scribner, 1970. Schoolhouse Press, 1998.

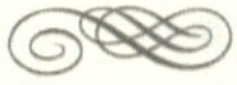

Walsh, Andrea, Cathi Charles Wherry, and Wil George. *Transporters I LECILEN: Contemporary Salish Art*. Victoria, BC: Art Gallery of Greater Victoria, 2007.

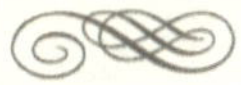

Welsh, Christine. *The Story of the Coast Salish Knitters*. Montreal, QC: National Film Board, 2008.

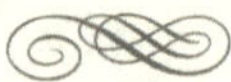

Winegard, Timothy C. *For King and Kanata: Canadian Indians and the First World War*. Winnipeg, MB: University of Manitoba Press, 2012.

Endnotes

1 Cook, James. *The Voyages of Captain Cook*, Vol. 2. London, UK: William Smith, 1842, p 263.

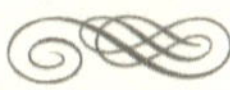

2 *Tough, girdled by mountains and approachable only by sea via Cape Horn or the Cape of Good Hope, that remote shore was of increasing interest to explorers, merchant traders, scientists, and governments. Its resources and lands encouraged an international rivalry, dating from the sixteenth century, that had important consequences with respect to establishing political boundaries on the Pacific coast of North America and with respect to changing the lives of native inhabitants – "Indians," Aleuts, and "Eskimos." The Northwest Coast was a dominion, a future sphere of empire, whose remoteness at once shaped its development and kept it secret from the wider world until the late eighteenth century* (Gough 4).

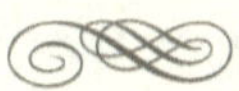

3 "The coastal migration theory has it that the first American colonisers moved into the continent from Beringia on watercraft by way of the Pacific northwest coast likely around 13,000 years B.P. or after," wrote Sara Perry in her Master's thesis. "Migrants

made use of existing shoreline 'refugia,' tucked amidst the deglaciating late Pleistocene landscape, for shelter and for rich non-marine food sources..." (Perry 85)

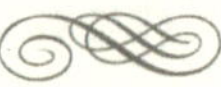

4 Vancouver, George. *A Voyage of Discovery to the North Pacific Ocean and Around the World.* John Vancouver, ed. London, UK: Stockdale, 1801, p 431.

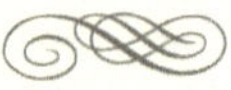

5 Gowlland, the second master on Richards's survey, kept journals of his own. In April 1860 Gowlland reported that in the Discovery Islands the ship's company would trade with the Indians, giving shirts for deer and "one large Elk I brought away in the pinnace could not have weighed less than 3cwt – for an old coat." (Dorricott and Cullon 39)

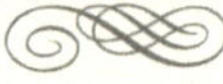

6 As Olsen observed, the shows were of more than local interest:

> *...in the early days of Vancouver Island exhibitions, knitting was categorized and judged based on the race of the knitter, and judges looking at the work of Coast Salish women examined how the knitters' technical skills measured up to the quality of the work done by settler women. In 1871 the judge at the Cowichan Agricultural Fair, invested with colonial condescension and keeping a watchful eye for signs of Indian "advancement," commented in the fair's report on "a very marked improvement in needlework [and] knitting." ... Coast Salish knitters' artistic innovations began to appear, and judges slowly came to recognize distinctly native*

characteristics. It was a few decades before the fusion of European skill and native design and industry took on a truly Coast Salish style. By the 1920s, in spite of its troubled categorization in the arts and crafts movement, Coast Salish knitting had become a favourite display item at the Cowichan agency booths at fairs and exhibitions around the world....Cowichan knitting had taken on a distinct and identifiable character of its own. So even though knitting was still shunned by art collectors and 'native' purists, Cowichan sweaters, in particular, were a marketable product because the distinct designs and unique patterns made them completely different from any other hand-knit – a cultural fusion yet at the same time a truly native innovation. In the end, Cowichan sweaters did not become popular with non-native people because of their artistic or tourist appeal or because Indian agents promoted them as examples of their civilizing successes but because they were warm and comfortable and they looked good to wear (Olsen 147).

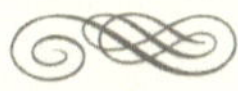

7 Meikle, Margaret. *Cowichan Indian Knitting*. Vancouver, BC: University of British Columbia Museum of Anthropology, 1987, p 4.

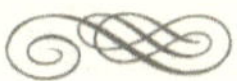

8 Olsen, Sylvia. *Working With Wool: A Coast Salish legacy & the Cowichan Sweater*. Winlaw, BC: Sono Nis, 2010, p144.

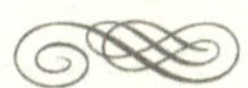

9 Kissell, Mary Lois. "A New Type of Spinning in North America." *American Anthropologist*, Vol. 18, April-June 1916, pp264-270.

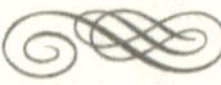

10 Johnston, Olive L. "Pioneer Woman's Gift to the Cowichans." *Family Herald: Canada's Farm Magazine*, No. 6 February 6, 1962, p34.

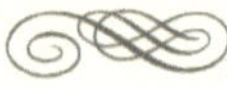

11 MacPherson, Jena. "Cowichan Sweaters." *Sunset magazine*, Fall 1996. Seattle, WA: Pacific Northwest Travel Guide, p18.

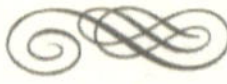

12 "The arts are not just a nice thing to have or to do if there is free time or if one can afford it," stated Michelle Obama at the Metropolitan Museum in 2009. "Rather, paintings and poetry, music and fashion, design and dialogue, they all define who we are as a people and provide an account of our history for the next generation."

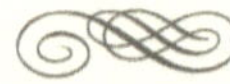

13 "I find a great importance in keeping traditional designs alive," said Scandinavian fibre professional Annemor Sundbø in an interview.

They belong to a universal symbol language. Most knitters regard a design as something to please the eye, but motifs and ornament are communication without spoken language, without borders or taboos. Traditional knitting is handed over from a time when the knitted items were gifts, amulets, and protection not only against weather and wind, but also against the dark and evil...When design becomes a language for you after studying symbol, it is more and more exciting to 'read' the message. (Nargi 103)

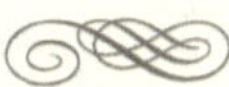

14 Hodgson, Sue. "Can We Talk? Sylvia Olsen, Author, Designer, On-Reserve Housing Technician." *Seaside Times: Your West Coast Culture*, July 2012. Sidney, BC: Rhino Print Solutions, pp 10-11.

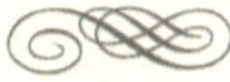

15 Faust joined the resistance against the Nazis, and as a Red Cross journalist was able to continue to exercise her writing and design talents during and after the Second World War, and after her emigration to Canada in 1953. As fibre arts writer Joe Lewis commented in his biographical essay on Faust, "Her work was filled with motifs and designs taken from ethnographic sources and art history that depicted elements of nature, flowers, trees and animals – images that continued to be foremost in her design and artwork for the rest of her life" (Lewis n.p).

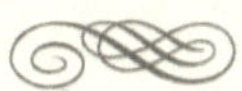

16 For reasons of space, this paper will not discuss the sale of imitation versions of Cowichan style sweaters at the 2010 Olympics in Vancouver, nor the arrests of Cowichan knitters

protesting the sale at the Olympics of imitation Cowichan-style sweaters machine-made in China. Both matters deserve thorough discussion.

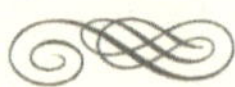

17 Hill, Tom. "Introduction." *American Indian Designs Adapted To Knitting*, by Regine Faust. Toronto, ON: Regine Studio, 1980.

Don't miss out!

Visit the website below and you can sign up to receive emails whenever Paula Johanson publishes a new book. There's no charge and no obligation.

https://books2read.com/r/B-A-ZKUK-UJJSB

BOOKS 2 READ

Connecting independent readers to independent writers.

Did you love *Woolgathering: Awareness of the Foreign in Published Works About Cowichan Woolworking*? Then you should read *King Kwong: Larry Kwong, the China Clipper Who Broke the NHL Colour Barrier*[1] by Paula Johanson!

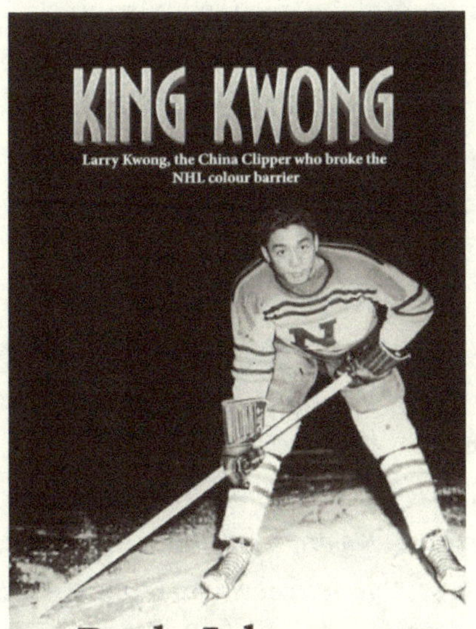

[2]

Who broke the colour barrier in the NHL? A man whose professional hockey career statistics include leading the senior leagues for scoring and for low penalty minutes -- and a single shift on the ice in an NHL game. He was scouted three times by NHL teams before that game, and courted away from the NHL to a powerful role in three different international leagues before retiring.

---

1. https://books2read.com/u/bOX6oA

2. https://books2read.com/u/bOX6oA

He is Larry Kwong, a Canadian of Chinese heritage born in Vernon BC in 1923, a hard-working man and World War II serviceman who played hockey most of his life.

Author Paula Johanson explores the life and accomplishments of the China Clipper, Larry Kwong. His story is one of an indomitable spirit who triumphs in the face of adversity and social discrimination. In 2013, Kwong was inducted into the BC Sports Hall of Fame as a pioneer.

"If you're not familiar with Larry Kwong, prepare to be amazed. This game-changing hero should be a household name in Canada and the hockey world. His inspiring story is one for the ages, yet it's still not widely known.

Author Paula Johanson brings justice to Kwong's extraordinary life. All the elements of classic fiction are here, and yet this is riveting history. We follow the ultimate long shot as he chases the 'impossible'...and triggers a shift in his society.

Johanson retraces Kwong's trailblazing strides with dexterity and grace. It's a mythic journey. From underclass underdog, he emerges as a larger-than-life hero. Transported, we can cheer on King Kwong as he smashes stereotypes and barriers with uncommon skill and class.

This is a long-overdue but timeless biography—a spellbinding tale of a puck magician whose escape from opposition checks and societal chains helped to recast a fairer future for us all."

- Chad Soon, Director, Greater Vernon Museum & Archives and Okanagan Sports Hall of Fame.

Doublejoy Books is pleased to present this fine biography, *King Kwong*, previously released by Five Rivers Publishing. This new edition includes an afterword by Chad Soon.

Read more at books2read.com/paulaj.

Also by Paula Johanson

Prime Ministers of Canada

Pierre Elliott Trudeau: Child of Nature

Charles Tupper: Warhorse

Slice of Life

No Parent Is An Island

Young Science

Bat Poop Sparkles

Standalone

Small Rain and Other Nightmares

Island Views

Plum Tree

Tower in the Crooked Wood

King Kwong: Larry Kwong, the China Clipper Who Broke the NHL Colour Barrier

Woolgathering: Awareness of the Foreign in Published Works About Cowichan Woolworking

Science Critters

Green Paddler

Watch for more at books2read.com/paulaj.

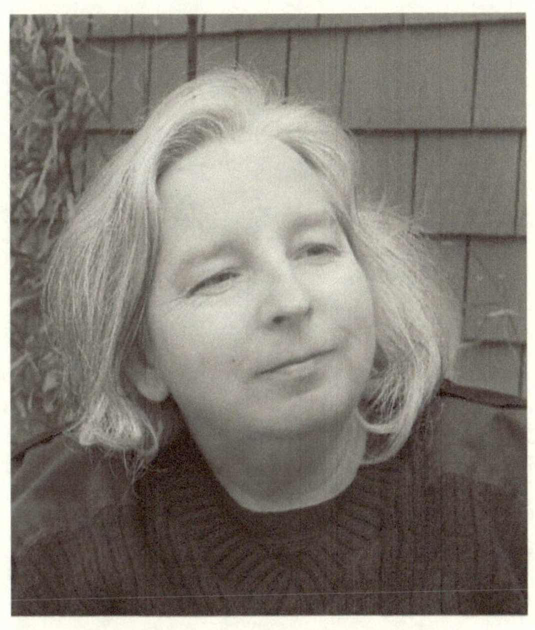

About the Author

Paula Johanson is a Canadian writer. A graduate of the University of Victoria with an MA in Canadian literature, she has worked as a security guard, a short order cook, a teacher, newspaper writer, and more. As well as editing books and teaching materials, she has run an organic-method small farm with her spouse, raised gifted twins, and cleaned university dormitories. In addition to novels and stories, she is the author of forty-two books written for educational publishers, among them *The Paleolithic Revolution* and *Women Writers* from the series *Defying Convention: Women Who Changed The World*. Johanson is an active member of SF Canada, the national association of science fiction and fantasy authors.

Read more at books2read.com/paulaj.

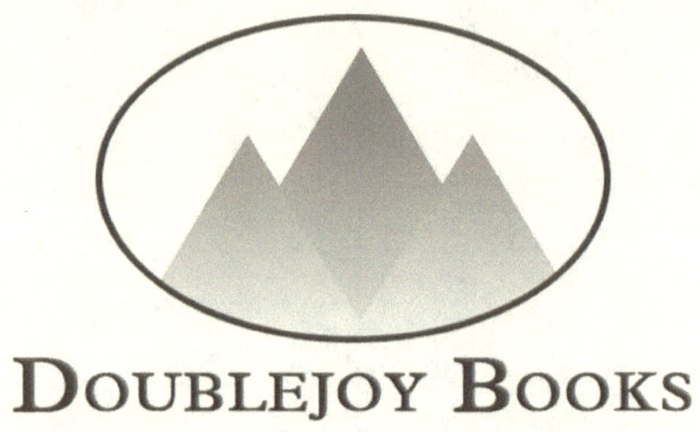

About the Publisher

Doublejoy Books is the publisher of a variety of eclectic books of Canadian literature.

http://doublejoybooks.com

http://books2read.com/paulaj

www.ingramcontent.com/pod-product-compliance
Lightning Source LLC
La Vergne TN
LVHW050942080826
845145LV00004B/1377

* 9 7 8 1 9 8 9 9 6 6 3 1 0 *